SEDUCTIVE
INTERIORS

SERA HERSHAM-LOFTUS

I dedicate this book to my three children who grew
up with their mum learning her craft.
Jacob, Anoushka Florence, and Gabriel.
And to my mentor, Rachel Ashwell.

Published in 2012 by CICO Books
An imprint of Ryland Peters & Small
519 Broadway, 5th Floor, New York NY 10012
20–21 Jockey's Fields, London WC1R 4BW
www.cicobooks.com

10 9 8 7 6 5 4 3 2 1

A CIP catalog record for this book is available from the Library of Congress and
the British Library.

ISBN: 978-1-908170-77-4

Printed in China

Editor: Hilary Mandleberg
Designer: Matthew Lake
Illustration: Jayne Pope
Specially commissioned photography: Gisela Torres
and Gavin Kingcome (pages 48–65)

CONTENTS

CHOCOLATE TOWERS
THE RECORDS

"Seductive, to me, signifies a person, a place, or a moment that, once encountered, I would not want to leave."

My name is Sera Hersham-Loftus aka "Madame Sera." I don't like to call myself an "interior designer" but rather an "interior decorator." The essence of my work is simple—it's a heady mix of romanticism, passion, and playfulness. I like to live in a loose, informal style that is reflected in my interiors. I don't buy anything for homes that is madly expensive. On the contrary, most of my furnishings come from flea markets or vintage stores. My look is essentially a concoction of enchanting soft lighting, charming antique and bohemian furnishings, oriental bric-a-brac, and more than a teaspoon of The Blues and Rock-'n'-Roll.

As you browse this book you will see "seductive interiors" that I have decorated and "seductive interiors" that I have been seduced by. This part of the book, The Records, is all about Chocolate Towers, my own house and "experimental launch pad" for new ideas. I painted it a deep chocolate brown on the outside and as it's tall, I refer to it (rather tongue in cheek) as a tower block— hence the name Chocolate Towers. It has grown from being a home for me and my three young children, Jacob, Anoushka, and Gabriel, to standing at the very heart of my craft as an interior decorator. It is also the haven that has waved the children off on their own creative paths.

Over the years, I have dressed the salons and boudoirs, scullery, and parlor of Chocolate Towers in different guises according to the different stages of my life. I feel passionate about moving the energy around in my rooms. You will see them all here in The Records.

Opposite Yours truly sitting for the legendary photographer, Clive Arrowsmith. He is not only the world's greatest fashion photographer, but has also photographed the Dalai Lama over the decades. Clive and his beautiful girlfriend Olenka are my greatest and oldest friends. One night over dinner, Clive suggested taking my portrait with me lying on my bed among my favorite fabrics, all folded and draped as in a Leonardo da Vinci painting.

MY SUMMER
ATTIC BOUDOIR

When I bought Chocolate Towers, the attics housed the water tanks and were split into two rather pokey rooms. I hid the tanks in the laundry room in the basement and opened up the entire attic floor to create one big bedroom with exposed beams and some exposed brickwork. I laid a waxed rubber floor that feels like velvet to walk on and I whitewashed the walls. It is my favorite bedroom in the entire world. I change its look with the seasons and, indeed, with my moods.

Above I curtained my bed in white Indian muslin, covered it with a golden Victorian piano shawl, and piled on a tumbling mass of pillows covered in antique Provençal linen pillowslips.

Opposite The gold satin deep-buttoned couch was made for me by my boyfriend of the time. It floats in the middle of the room with a Balinese parasol and an Indian screen providing privacy for anyone bathing in the copper bathtub. Shell decorations and ferns dangle from the rafters. At this stage of my life, my house was a desert island hideaway. I would light Indian incense and play Nitin Sawhney and Anoushka Shankar.

THE VICTORIAN PARLOR & SCULLERY

The photograph on the left was taken in the Victorian parlor when we had just moved in. It shows my Chesterfield sofa before I started to patchwork it. I loved the Victorian "bordello" look back then. Note how all the furnishings lean toward a slightly louche vibe.

I found the stone sink in the photograph above at an architectural salvage yard. Back in the day it was used for washing clothes, but now it gives me a flamboyant excuse for leaving the washing up as long as possible since I can stack dozens of pans and plates in it. It must be the bachelor in me! I house my cooking pans under the sink, disguising them with curtains made from antique linen sheets that I found in a market. Some even have delightful old monograms on them. My neighbor and dear friend Philip Sallon draped ivy over the mirror above the sink for this photograph while I boiled the water for our tea.

Above is a view through to my conservatory on the ground floor during my Native American phase. It was a steaming summer when I arrived back from the Burning Man music festival in Nevada's Black Rock Desert. All the girls strolled around in cowboy hats with feathers in their hair, wearing chamois leather ponchos and fringed shawls and boots. It proved the inspiration for me to create my very own Native American look at home.

On the right we are back on the top floor in my Attic Boudoir. The window shutters and the surround for my new bathtub are made from carved pierced screens from Rajasthan. I have hung a fringed gypsy shawl at the window, and the bathtub is flanked on either side with boxwood ball hedges in muslin-covered pots. The Moroccan-style rug edged in silver sequins is by fashion designer Liza Bruce.

MY GILDED WORKROOM

This workroom—and occasional dining room and mini parlor—has been gessoed and gilded by my artist-in-residence Miss Jayne Pope to look like an antique piece of furniture. The room is lit by beautiful crystal lanterns. On the left is my old shirtmaker's cabinet housing my ribbons and fabrics. I stenciled the floor to resemble that of The Spanish Riding School in Vienna at the turn of the last century. Either side of the mirror, the two panels open to reveal closets that hold my books on art and literature.

THE VICTORIAN GOTHIC PARLOR

The front parlor is painted black with white baseboards and white plaster details. To the right of the hearth, the large photograph was an advert for crystal glassware that I had spotted in a store window display. When they changed the display, I bought the photo. The two white chairs are from Portobello market, West London's famous antique market. This photograph was taken by Colin Streater and styled by Mr Philip Sallon.

THE
PATCHWORK SOFA

I bought this beat-up 1930s sofa when the children were young. I chopped off its legs as
I prefer sitting low. I find it more relaxing. As the years have gone by, I have patched it up
in places where it needed mending. I have used leather from old motorbike jackets, lace
from vintage dresses, and velvets from old drapes found in flea markets. This sofa fits
with so many looks—Bordello, Exotic, Space Age, Africa. It's definitely going to be
passed down as a family heirloom. I often wonder how it will look in 20 years from now,
when it will belong to my children and when they have added patches to suit their own taste.
It's a very much-loved piece.

Above I was the interior decorator on Kimberly Stewart's TV show "Kimberly
Moves to London" and one night after filming, I captured her hanging out on
my Patchwork Sofa.

Opposite Here is the Patchwork Sofa in the Gothic Parlor. The "Biba Nude" above
the sofa is a vintage photograph by James Wedge that was produced as a poster.
These posters were to have appeared on London buses, but were banned. Again,
this photograph was taken by Colin Streater and styled by Mr Philip Sallon.

THE SUPERSTAR
SILVER SOFA

The 1970s silver deep-buttoned sofa has had Kate Moss, Amy Winehouse, and Lara Stone, to name a few, draped over it for the world's top fashion magazines. The sofa can easily be moved around the house for my room experiments. The ultra-moody feel in here makes this the "purrfect" late-night after-party hangout room.

MY GILDED WORKROOM

In another disguise—this time with my collection of intricately
embroidered piano shawls as drapes and chair coverings.

CHOCOLATE TOWERS
MY EXPERIMENTAL LAUNCH PAD

"Seductive interiors are what I sell—they're my stock in trade."

My home, Chocolate Towers, is my Experimental Launch Pad. It's the place where I try out new decorating ideas. For me, decorating is an art form and just as an artist needs to experiment with paint, so I need to experiment with decoration. I find it an intensely creative process to design a "new look," as Dior would have said.

My inspiration can be anything from an antique dress, a scrap of lace or fabric, a vintage handbag, or a battered old trunk replete with its original passage stickers. I generally don't have to wait too long before I see something that sparks my imagination—and then I'm off.

When my children were young, they became accustomed to coming back home after school to a newly decorated room. At one point this would happen almost on a daily basis.

My Experimental Launch Pad feeds my soul and gives my customers the opportunity to see my new room designs and my latest way of thinking.

Opposite A 1930s chaise longue holds court in my conservatory and a splendid Victorian mirror reflects the room facing. The lace Rude Lampshades light the scene while a Victorian crocheted pelmet frames the door opening.

THE HALLWAY

Here is a peek through candles and silver leather to
the White Room. The white sofa was a market find
and the silver chairs are from a 1970s disco.

PARISIAN ELEVATOR SHAFT

The balustrade was made for me by my metalworker friend as a moving-in gift. We had spent a weekend in Paris and were inspired by the magnificent ironwork elevators there. Inspiration became reality.

Two aspects of the conservatory show it dressed in my "Bohemian armor."

Above The 1930s lady's Chesterfield sofa is swathed in a fringed shawl and bedecked with one of my Foxy Cushions. Behind it, the picture of a scarlet woman is an early Victorian circus girl. The 1970s lampshade in front of the palms is made of cork.
Opposite My delectable conservatory with blooms of roses and palms.

I collect antique textiles and keep them in closets all over the house. Even in the kitchen, where one would expect to see flatware, the drawers brim with vintage buttons and the like. My collection allows me to change the look of the rooms constantly. Days when I replace fabrics that have been on display for a few months with different ones from my magnificent store, I call "fluffing up" days. Here my workshop looks splendid in red and white Toile de Jouy. An eighteenth-century window valance hides away all my everyday office clutter.

PEACE & CREAM

My bed, in the attic of The Towers, is a large mattress on the floor cloaked in an assortment of antique throws, frilly Rachel Ashwell bedcovers, and an abundance of my Foxy Cushions in faux leopard skin and satin. Floor-to-ceiling lace panels provide a veil of discretion between my bed and the bathing area, which is on the other side of the room. There is an open fire to one side and plants and musical instruments are dotted around.

"We wouldn't allow Sera to photograph the bedroom she designed for us because we feel bedrooms are private. However, I can say that, had she done so, you would have seen another of her exquisite fantasies created to make her clients feel they live part of the time in a chateau and part of the time in a bordello." Howard Jacobson

Left My Attic Boudoir is screened by lace and uplit palms. The 1970s cork lampshade sits on an Italian table while sitars and guitars lie casually around.

Overleaf My bath sits at the other end of my boudoir. A Fortuny silk chandelier hangs above it and plants and flowers flank it on either side. Dressing screens from the 1930s become a "closet" and an enormous pile of books sits on the floor. The Emmanuelle chair awaits my "undressing" in this stunningly romantic scene. As in the bedroom half, I have used vintage laces as subtle screening. Although see-through, they still bring a sense of separation to the room.

DRIPPING LACE POWDER ROOM

No larger than a minute, my powder room is a stepping stone away from my boudoir. There is no room for a bathtub— only for a washbasin and a dainty lady's chair—so I like to call it my "Poudre Room d'Amour." I have papered it from head to toe in my Dripping Lace wallpaper.

Left The cherub detail of the wall sconce.
Opposite The Victorian gilded and mirrored wall sconce is adorned with my jewelry, candles, and postcards from my children and friends.

THE KITCHEN

Our family kitchen is the heart and soul of Chocolate Towers. Beyond the curtained double doors lies my magical herb garden. The eighteenth-century oak refectory table brims with character and charm. It has certainly borne witness to a great many stories, some of which I wouldn't even dare to recall. Flanking the double doors, a pair of antique armchairs sits under plaster-framed mirrored sconces, while a Colonial Indian ceiling fan purrs gently overhead, creating a refreshing breeze through this entire cooking milieu.

Above An ivory kitchen range sits in the original fireplace with its massive heraldic plaster mantelpiece overhead. On either side I built a pair of nooks out of reclaimed white-painted bricks. They store glassware and have concealed lighting inside. I have so many glasses because my favorite pastime is giving parties at Chocolate Towers.
Opposite In the scullery area, an overmantel mirror—now bereft of its ivy trim—sits proudly above the massive stone sink. Antique linen curtains pegged to wires hide the pots, pans, and even the dishwasher. The kitchen walls are painted a very simple off-white.

Overleaf Left The dainty armoire is filled with white china and even more glassware. The checkerboard floor leads through to the garden room. Nickel radiators give a slight edge to "ye olde scullery."
Overleaf Right Tasseled upholstery braid edges shelves holding pots of herbs and my cookery and travel books.

SOFT FOCUS
SALONS

THE
GIRL NEXT DOOR
Nina Gill

THE
ART STUDENT
Anoushka Florence Loftus

THE
TONY AWARD WINNER
Frances Ruffelle

THE
POET
Lily-India

THE
SHOW GAL
Esmé

THE
GIRL NEXT DOOR
NINA GILL

Growing up, I had a fantasy about decorating the overgrown, rambling Georgian house that was next to my parents' home. So, when, I received a phone call from the new owner appointing me as her interior decorator, I was overjoyed. Nina Gill, a Malaysian beauty, gave me a brief that consisted of the following: "I want to live in a light and airy haven, so that when I come home I feel like I have been transported to another world."

To fulfil that brief I created a calm but inspiring palette of varying degrees of white. Each room is painted a slightly different tone of white to the next, with blushes of soft colour added here and there.

During the day, when the sun comes streaming in, the house is a light, diaphanous space. At night or on dull days, the mood lighting I devised creates a magical sense of being on a tropical hideaway desert island.

All my commissioned balustrades are by the artist and metalworker, Andrew Findlay. This one is brushed metal with an antiqued blue-green patina to it that looks as if it has been aging gracefully at Nina's house forever. The design is made up of huge clusters of overgrown, bursting grapes on a never-ending vine that travels up and down the house in a tailored yet unruly fashion.

Left The magnificent balustrade made by Andrew Findlay.
Opposite A pair of antique Italian chairs sit beneath lace-covered lamps in front of a waterfall of glorious lace drapes and drapery.

Overleaf The light from the gently glowing lace-covered lamps reflects off the gilded wood of the armchairs and the sequined cushions on the sofa. The sofa has a loose cover made of washable white denim from Rachel Ashwell's store, Shabby Chic Couture. The more you wash the denim, the softer it becomes.

SOFT FOCUS
LIGHTING

▸ ▸ ▸ ▸ ▸ ▸ ▸ ▸ ▸ ▸ ▸ ▸

I feel that lighting a room is a little like conducting an orchestra. Once all the lights are in place, they just need to be adjusted by the conductor according to the mood that's required.

For Nina's house I created three different lighting sources, which are all on my *de rigueur* dimmers.

They are wall-lights, floor lamps, and hidden uplights for Nina's collection of plants, pictures, and sculptures. Most of the uplights emit the usual clear halogen light, but in the reception rooms I used amber bulbs, which give a gorgeous, warm glow that resembles candlelight.

I designed the lighting to all be on at the same time, but the moodiness comes into play and the sense of being transported to another world is felt when the dimmers are "tweaked."

The wall-lights are rather like lanterns softly framing the walls. They are made from the finest lingerie laces and are trimmed with crystals salvaged from antique chandeliers. When they are on, they create a wonderful hazy and diffused, delicate light.

The floor lamps give a lower level of light, which is also akin to candlelight. These are my Rude Lampshades. I fashioned them to look like witty Victorian bustiers, which add a touch of classy humor to the rooms.

The secret of the flattering light they give out lies in the lampshade linings. I hand-dye them a kind of peachy nude color in my bathtub at home. Their light makes everyone in the room appear beautiful, seeming to give them a flawless complexion.

The leaves of the uplit plants create beautiful shadows on the ceiling both at night and during the day. They add a bit of "nature's seduction" to the room.

So there is my orchestra ready and waiting to be fine-tuned by the conductor as the mood takes her.

Left The vestibule with its delicate lighting.

DISGUISED TV
& DEEPLY
BEGUILING SALON

I gave Nina the option of disguising the plasma screen in her salon with a theatrical, stage-curtain-like panel made of ribbons of white raffia. Another identical panel below hides all the TV and DVD paraphernalia. The curtains close when the set is not on. The panels add some playful mystery and fun to the room.

The window drapes are all made from translucent fabrics so the light can come through them, but they still provide privacy from the street. I used dress fabrics such as organza and lace and made them so they just kiss the floor. There is a simple white privacy blind behind each pair for night-time use.

Right The TV nook in the salon.

Overleaf It is always important to buy or commission pieces for a home that will age and become more beautiful over time. For Nina I chose furniture that is a mix of classic chic and antiques that one would usually find in a romantic family-owned hotel in Italy. Here a gilded Italian table and chair sit in the window of the salon with an ornate white-painted armoire.

NINA'S BOUDOIR

Nina wanted a peachy look in her bedroom, so rather than paint it one color, we built up layers and layers of ochers, yellows, peaches, and reds. This technique is almost like lacquering, creating a depth of color and movement that makes it feel like the walls have always been like this and gives them that beautiful patina that one only sees in old Tuscan palazzos.

Around the bed I suspended four panels of organza on wire, creating a four-poster effect but without the poles. It's a simple and much lighter look.

Nina's 1930s headboard is deep-buttoned in an amaretto-colored satin and I covered the pair of slipper chairs from the same era in fabric to match. The windows are draped with white silk satin that falls like a dream onto the waxed rubber floors that are like velvet to walk on.

The dressing-room screen is draped with a vintage piano shawl and I have used my signature Indian fretwork as closet doors.

The lighting in the bedroom is gentle with table lights and floor lamps made, as before, from lingerie laces.

Right Mrs M Baker made the silk satin curtains that frame the windows overlooking the street. The piano shawl and stool add a flash of contrasting strawberry, and the satin-covered chairs glow in the light.

Overleaf A view from Nina's "four-poster" bed looking through to her dressing area. I made the lace lampshades that cast their glow over Nina's golden satin chairs.

THE GILDED STUDY
& THE WRITING ROOM

All the rooms in Nina's home have working fireplaces and all the fireplaces have gas fires. I love the real deal but from a practical point of view, gas is so easy. If you want it, you push a button, if you don't, you simply push another one.

I find a gas fire with coals looks more realistic than one with fake logs—and the more coals the better. To look natural the coals should tumble down on top of each other, as if the coals underneath are burning away and the top ones are replacing them.

These two rooms both have fibrous plaster panels that I had gilded to give a look of splendor. Small rooms like these can take an over-the-top treatment and still look charming, while big rooms with the same treatment can verge on the "flash" side of decor.

These rooms both have the same floor treatment. Miss Jayne Pope, stenciled the original wooden floors to create a kind of Alice In Wonderland overscaled look in a small space.

Opposite A delightful vintage sofa set upholstered in embossed cranberry satin and deep-buttoned white linen encircles the fireplace in the Gilded Study.

Overleaf The Writing Room has duck-egg blue walls set with gilded plaster panels, crystal lamps, and a ceramic mirror by the artist Oriel Harwood.

How do you catch a pink star and pin it down? My daughter Anoushka Loftus is a university art student who studies in Miami. When she comes home on her holidays I am spiritually uplifted. She is like a bolt of bubbling pink lightning. She is the most exciting company as a daughter and a friend. Her love of art and people have led her to curating art exhibitions in South Beach, discovering unknown artists, and putting them on her map for her future travels. Her love of pink since she was a child is evident in her choice of room colors and indeed her shoe collections.

Above Anoushka and Gabriel Loftus.

Opposite Anoushka's shoes are a mix of hand-me-down vintage Terry de Havilland, and retro shoes, boots, and sneakers.

Overleaf Not for the faint-hearted. Anoushka's clashing pink pillows are thrown onto the vast curved bed that almost fills the entire room. My ubiquitous Indian screens and vintage textiles add a calming element.

One spring day I was approached by Frances Ruffelle, the extra-ordinarily talented stage siren, to help her decorate her gorgeous mews (originally stables) house in London's Primrose Hill.

She wanted it sexy, bohemian, and cozy. The more I have come to know her, the more I realize that what she wanted for her home was, subconsciously, a true reflection of herself.

Frankie is like a star out of a Fellini movie. She is a world-renowned talent as a singer, actress, and dancer. She is also a ravishing beauty with smoldering femme-fatale looks (there have been comparisons to Anouk Aimée, the 1960s actress). On top of that, she has a dangerous giggle that is madly infectious.

We are now great pals. We both have three almost grown-up children about whom we are passionate. Her daughter is the poptastic Eliza Doolittle (see pages 114–119), her son Nat is a magnificent artist, and her other son Felix is a budding musician. We are both addicted to life, love, and friends, and we share the ethos that a home should not be precious but should be a retreat and a sanctuary for all who live there and all who visit.

*"Sera is the most stylish woman
I have ever met. Her sexy interiors
reflect a joie de vivre that she and I
share. They are crazily romantic and
riotously decadent but still have a real
sophistication and class that only she
can pull off."*
Frances Ruffelle

Frances has an abundant collection of candlesticks and she lights candles at nightfall in every possible corner of the house.

To light Frances's beaten-up characterful refectory table (bought from an antique dealer in Chelsea), we chose glass-and-nickel lanterns. These can be used with either amber or clear lightbulbs, but they also have candleholders perched at the end of their arms, which makes for a doubly dramatic effect.

Frankie is the most superb cook. She religiously cooks a full English breakfast and a proper dinner every night thats she's at home. I have shared many out-of-this-world meals with her and the table has played host to huge numbers of gregarious, scintillating people.

Opposite A crude refectory table laid with Primrose Hill cupcakes and other finery. African rugs soften the floor.

Overleaf Left & Right Frankie collects desks and armoires. These are hand-carved mahogany. The desk displays favorite books and pictures. The Arts and Crafts cabinet holds her collection of antique clothing and things of sentimental value that she has amassed from her trips around the globe.

FRANKIE'S
GYPSY BOUDOIR

▸ ▸ ▸ ▸ ▸ ▶ ▸ ◂ ▸ ◂ ▸ ◂ ◂

I love the romance of a gypsy lifestyle, and Frankie's under-the-eaves boudoir reflects this. We filled the vast space with one enormous floor mattress and I made her a divinely dainty bedcover out of vintage lace panels and hand-painted white velvet curtains that we found together in Portobello market. On top of the bed we placed oversized frilly pillows from my favorite London shop, Shabby Chic Couture. The back of the bed is backlit with a glorious golden light.

An ebonized egg-shaped bathtub sits on the white floorboards like a delightful Thai canoe. Here she and her lover can bathe together or take turns, while the other lolls around on the bed reading, resting, waiting ...

Right Tranquility rules in Frankie's gypsy boudoir. The bathtub is filled with scented bubbles and scattered rose petals.

THE
ROOF TERRACE

The roof terrace that overlooks the antiquated terra-cotta chimneypots, old TV aerials, and slate tiles of the neighbors' roofs is reminiscent of days gone by. Frankie has whitewashed the exposed bricks. and the delicate Victorian ironwork table and chairs were found at a market.

Every time I stand here I have a real "Mary Poppins moment." Pigeons and swallows fly overhead and the sound of nothing but woodcocks and owls makes me believe we are living in Victorian times. I can almost hear the horses trotting on the cobbled streets below.

This is a gem of a home; a real treasure chest with a family that matches up to each and every breath of its beauty.

THE POET
LILY-INDIA

The poet living here is in every possible sense a true romantic. She wanted a "lost in love" type of vibe for her family home in Primrose Hill. I created a gessoed effect paint finish on her walls and added gilded panels which I had specially made out of fibrous plaster. To light the rooms I made a collection of Rude Lampshades using fabulous vintage lingerie fabrics.

Above The poet Lily-India's writing desk, where many a poem has been penned.
Opposite A Florentine lace curtain hangs in front of Lily's bedroom door.

Overleaf Left Lacy Rude Lampshades light the gilded and gessoed hallways.
Overleaf Right I made a lady's sofa to fit inside this nook.

r door—coughing a little

scent--Esmé arose from

quired about my interior

ration. After a brief

ired to decorate her fancy,

ooms in Shoreditch.

oted was how I imagined a

s Pullman railway carriage

o the air of languor and

ested she keep her heating

light fires in the summer.

found a 1930s peach satin

a inspired me to make a

each and powder blue

Foxy Cushions trimmed

thers, sequins, and pearls.

pear yet again as window

vere painted roughly with

Not The Orient Express but "The Oriental Dive." The bed is hung with faded antique gold velvet curtains from a turn-of-the-century Italian palazzo that I bought at auction in Rome. I made Esmé a collection of faux leopard skin and silk damask cushions to bedeck the bed. Pampas grasses, feathers, and palms waft aloft and Esmé's unmistakable perfumes scent the air, adding to the intoxicating scene.

"LOLLING POWER"

Satin eau-de-nil curtains drape this bed and Foxy Cushions
stuffed with lavender give more "lolling" power to all who
hang out here.

MOODY &
MAGNIFICENT
PARLORS

THE
ACTRESS
Sadie Frost

THE
BALLERINA
Naomi Tate

THE
POP IDOL
Eliza Doolittle

THE
MILLINER
Victoria Grant

THE
IMPRESARIO
Mr David Carter

THE
HEDONISTIC
HAVEN
A child's dream

THE ACTRESS
SADIE FROST

There is something dreamy and otherworldy about the British actress Sadie Frost. She appears so vulnerable, undiscovered, and yet somehow modest. Her almost gothic pale skin is set off by her legendary eyes; they are huge—like deep smoky pools in which one could get lost. Sadie is also dignified and ladylike and with her cupid-bow lips, she sits up there alongside silent-movie stars such as Clara Bow and Sarah Bernhardt.

Every time we meet, I never fail to be impressed by her strength and sensuality as a woman, mother, and friend. She is the old-fashioned matriarch of her exquisite family of four children. She is also a doyenne of style, both in her fashion sense and her taste in interiors.

This is one truly bohemian, yet ultra-sophisticated, grounded lady. A lady who has lived the wild life with its hedonistic, free and hazy days, and has come out the other side more beautiful and sexy, wiser, and stronger. She is a *tour de force*.

"Sera's style and designs caught my eye because they are so beautiful, so boudoir, so clever and so detailed. Her look is exotic, from a time long gone or an old movie set. Her designs fit so perfectly with my taste, complementing but not dictating. She is a true talent, a rock 'n' roll rebel of design who breaks rules with her originality and depth."
Sadie Frost

Above A portrait of Sadie by Jake and Dinos Chapman.
Opposite Sadie among her Foxy Cushions playing with her pooch, Rosie.

Sadie's exquisite home oozes class and taste. Beautiful photographs of her with her gorgeous family and superstar friends line the staircase walls.

In among this splendid collage is a magnificent black-and-white photograph of Sadie with film director Francis Ford Coppola on the set of the 1992 film *Dracula*. There is also a portrait in oils of her by Jake and Dinos Chapman, and photographs of her family that have been framed like works of art.

A loose vibe pervades the house. Her very beautiful children are ensconced with either friends, tutors, dogs, TV's, or Game Boys.

Sadie is a visionary, her taste is sophisticated, super-groovy, and glamorous, all in the same breath. She has made her home a sanctuary for anyone who enters.

Above A portrait of Sadie and her business partner, Jemima French, by Tim Watkins.
Left A portrait of Sadie on the set of *Dracula* with Francis Ford Coppola.
Opposite Photographs of Sadie and friends line the staircase walls.

Sadie's Boulevard-Strip-cum-Biba-Babe bathroom, bedroom, and dressing room, set behind a large pair of Victorian double doors, feel very private, almost cut off from the family home.

Darkness pervades apart from shafts of light filtering through the ebony-stained plantation shutters. The light illuminates the breathtaking ensemble of furnishings, books, objects, and vintage clothing.

A 1930s mirrored dressing table, laden with fancy perfume bottles and exquisite cut flowers from Sadie's garden, helps to bounce the light around the rooms.

Bruised plum walls and dark oak floors create the frame for the magnificent polished mahogany, intricately carved four-poster bed. Leopard-skin cushions adorn the bed, which is casually draped with marabou capes, feather boas, and vintage chiffon tea dresses. Sadie uses her collection of Louis Vuitton luggage as side tables to display her divine shoes and hats of the moment.

Entering Sadie's home is like witnessing some stolen romantic moment from a long-gone Gatsby era. It is ultra-seductive and elegantly bohemian—just like Sadie herself.

Above Tealights illuminate figurines, flowers, and foliage on Sadie's glamorous dressing table.
Opposite Taking pride of place at the bathroom window is a neon Boulevard Strip sign conjuring up the faded glitz and glamor of past times. A fake fur rug covers the floor while ferns, palms, and scarlet gladioli complete the 1960s Biba-Babe effect.

THE BALLERINA
NAOMI TATE

I'll never forget the first time I encountered the languid charms of the divine Naomi Tate. I was introduced to her by an artist friend who suggested I go to see Naomi's exquisite collection of handmade chokers and cuffs that she designs using vintage lace and rare gems.

I arrived promptly at Naomi's house at 4pm one summer's afternoon. I was totally unprepared for the ravishing beauty who opened the door. She reminded me of one of the models photographed by Deborah Turbeville in the 1970s. Naomi boasts the reddest curls tumbling down to her waist, the purest alabaster skin I have ever seen, and the smokiest, most beguiling temptress eyes.

Formerly a highly gifted ballerina, Naomi danced worldwide with The American Ballet Theatre and was known particularly for her dramatic, lyrical qualities.

Now she divides her time between acting, designing fabulous interiors, and devising her collections of beautiful adornments as she whiles away the time between takes.

As we sat and talked in her wildly romantic rooms that overlook the extraordinary communal gardens, my eyes traveled languorously around her salon replete with faded, crumbling antique curtains, velvet screens, Fortuny textiles, and old plaster walls, evocative of a faded Italian Palazzo.

The more I looked, the more captivated I was by her beauty and by her enchanting home reminiscent of Rosetti painting.

Opposite A portrait of Naomi by Gail Hadani is the backdrop to Naomi's collection of handmade chokers.

Overleaf Left A decaying silk damask curtain looks completely at home next to the peeling plaster walls. One of my Rude Lampshades perches on a gilded cabriole-leg side table.

Overleaf Right A trio of handcarved candleholders stands in front of a Venetian screen covered in Fortuny fabric. The gentle glow from a wall-light illuminates a painting in a gilt frame and a red and white marble fireplace.

"In Sera I have found a kindred spirit. She is a romantic and a reveler in all things beautiful, be they Fortuny fabrics, my vintage chokers, her lingerie lace lampshades, or simply an old, crumbling wall."
Naomi Tate

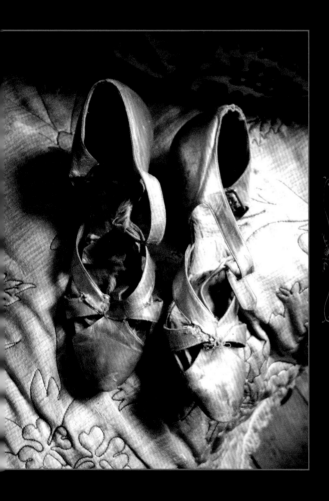

Preceding Page Massive windows in Naomi's Italian palazzo-style drawing room overlook the wild communal gardens.

Above A pair of Naomi's vintage walking shoes.
Right A shabby Aubusson tapestry covers the drawing room sofa, with a Venetian hanging pinned onto the wall above. A gilded chair and a vintage metal garden chair stand guard.

Overleaf Left Swathes of glorious Venetian silks shroud the daybed in Naomi's study, with a painted screen bedecked with irises behind.
Overleaf Right A branch from a contorted willow is a splendid display stand for Naomi's straw hats in her library.

MOODY & MAGNIFICENT PARLORS

THE POP IDOL
ELIZA DOOLITTLE

One summer's day, I received a phone call that earned me the honorary title of "Fairy Godmother" to the pop idol Eliza Doolittle. The call was from my friend and Eliza's mother, Frances Ruffelle. She wanted me to help realize Eliza's dream—the decoration of Eliza's Camden Town apartment—while Eliza was away on her first world tour.

Eliza is one of the greatest pop stars that our country has produced in recent years. Her music is ultra-upbeat and super-groovy, just like her. As well as being known for her music, her Amazonian figure and Byzantine beauty have brought her renown in the world of modeling too.

Before Eliza left for her tour, we spoke about what she wanted for her apartment, and she was very definite about the color palette, design, and feel of it. Her everyday clothes are young and fun-loving and she was looking for a similar vibe for her home—vivid shades of hot pinks, mad purples, and soft lilacs. She had grown up in the most colorful of environments so anything white was not an option.

Eliza has such an inimitable style that I know she will start trends in the interior design world just as she has started them in the worlds of music and fashion.

"I met Sera at her home and could see how strongly her character is reflected there. I looked around and the detail simply blew my mind. I said to myself, 'I want a home just like that someday.' So when it came to decorating my little apartment, I really wanted her to help me make it my own. Sera was incredible. She sourced things that I would never have been able to find, and gave me ideas that I would never have thought of. I am totally in love with it!" Eliza Doolittle

Opposite I covered Eliza's bed with my Foxy Cushions, made up in some of her favorite colors. Wall panels painted coral and bordered with green add an unexpected edginess as does the juxtaposition of the red-painted rattan headboard with the old-school mirror and the crystal wall-lights.

For her dressing room, Eliza chose my trademark Indian screens that I made into window shutters. I painted their frames a playful Moroccan sky-blue color. The handles are handmade carved wooden flowers made in India.

On the wall alongside, mini shelves edged in candy-pink pleated ribbon and dripping with glass beads provide display stands for Eliza's glitzy collection of amazing platform shoes.

ELIZA'S POPTASTIC LOVE PAD

Here in Eliza's salon, the sofa is weighed down with Foxy Cushions made from old Indian saris and 1970s satins and velvets. I found these fabrics on a rather successful flea-market day. Eliza added to the colorful assortment with her choice of lively Moroccan rugs for the floor.

Frances festooned the window with hand-dyed lace given to her by her mother, Sylvia Young, and then we hung long trails of Indian marigolds on top of fuchsia-pink muslin drapes. The result is that the room's natural light is colored a frisky hot pink.

Moroccan lanterns add to the vibe of a well-traveled home. Their gentle light contrasts with the neon pizzazz of the striking coffee table.

This room sums up Eliza—her spirit and her home—in just one word: "Love" in brightly blazing neon lights.

Right One afternoon, after eating freshly baked cheesecake and blinis at the Russian Tea Rooms just around the corner from Eliza's pad, Frankie dragged me into Daniel Poole's fantastic shop. Earlier that day she had spotted a 1960s coffee table that had more than winked at her. This handsome pop-art piece now takes pride of place in Eliza's colorful salon.

THE MILLINER
VICTORIA GRANT

> ▸ ▸ ▸ ▴ ▸ ▴ ▸ ▸ ◂ ▴ ▸ ▴ ▸ ▸ ▴ ◂ ▸

The superstar milliner, Victoria Grant, is a great friend of mine and is infused with an air of bubbly vivacity and dynamic spirit that is ever-present in her chic, characterful, and amusing hat designs. Her customers range from the British royal family to British rock royalty and, as one might expect, she wouldn't be seen dead without one of her swanky numbers planted firmly on her head.

It comes as no surprise to learn that Victoria's love of and inspiration for all things highly decorated began while she was growing up. Her father was a member of the bodyguard to the Lord Mayor of London, whose work attire consisted of uniforms from the reign of Charles I, right down to the feather-trimmed hats.

Victoria's home is a delicious old ballroom on the first floor of a Victorian house in Bayswater in West London. This home also acts as her extremely salubrious hat studio. It is where she creates her avant garde pieces and where her never-ending stream of well-heeled clients come for their fittings.

Victoria's floors are stenciled in a grand, exaggerated design fit for her ballroom of hats. I placed uplit *de rigueur* Kentia palms in all four corners of the room.

The walls have a tongue-in-cheek 1980s *trompe l'oeil* paint effect which I'm certain will be making a comeback soon. And where better to use it than as a backdrop to Victoria's new millennium hats?

When Victoria entertains, she does so surrounded by her hats. The house needs no further ornamentation. There are hats on stands, hats pinned to the walls, hats laid on tables. Some hats light up, others have neon signs attached. There are hats with clusters of cherries, hats with handmade flowers, hats with veiling, and hats with diamanté.

One can only compare these hat soirées to Holly Golightly's parties in *Breakfast at Tiffany's*. There you

will find London's most fashionable and flamboyant figures cutting a dashing scene framed by Victoria's tasteful hat displays in her eclectic showroom.

"Sera's genius interiors are like stepping into a world of magic. Her exotic, bohemian style does more than transform a space; it creates an atmosphere that conjures up a natural, relaxed rock 'n' roll way of living that you can only dream of. But Sera manages to deliver!"
Victoria Grant

Above A sprightly red cherry hat is embellished with sparkling sequins.
Opposite Victorious Victoria in fencing mood.

Overleaf The dining room laden with hats.

THE SALUBRIOUS HAT STUDIO

Hats adorn every available surface, showing that they can bejewel homes like pieces of art.

THE IMPRESARIO
MR DAVID CARTER

Sandwiched between the multicultural stores that line East London's Mile End Road in Stepney, where beautiful girls of all cultures walk side by side, wearing yashmaks, saris, ghetto gear, and Gucci, and the noise and fumes of buses, trucks, and cars are quite overwhelming, stands a splendid terrace of Edwardian brick houses. One of these gems is the home of one of my more eccentric friends, the interior decorator Mr David Carter.

David and I met many moons ago when he came to Chocolate Towers to commission a collection of Rude Lampshades for his Stepney home.

I had seen David's extraordinary work on the cover of *World of Interiors*. He had decorated a dentist's waiting room in France in the most flamboyant manner. So even before we met, I was very aware of his enormous talent.

His tongue is as sharp as Oscar Wilde's and he cuts a very tall, very thin figure with almost anemic-looking white skin. With an appearance that has on many occasions been compared to that of the actor John Hurt, David has modeled for Italian Vogue and various of the out-there glossies.

His everyday wear is a concoction of vintage clothing, Vivienne Westwood, and Yohji Yamamoto, all of which hang on him as if they were tailor-made. Consistently very well groomed, David is the true epitome of a dapper, old-fashioned Englishman.

"Sera's interiors are deliciously fun, dreamy, and very, very sexy."
Mr David Carter

Opposite David's chinoiserie-inspired front parlor has a stunning backdrop of hand-painted De Gournay wallpaper.

Overleaf Left In the kitchen, a magnificent handmade marble inlaid countertop and handmade wallpaper bear witness to their owner's eccentricity.

Overleaf Right A seductive walkway leads into a surprisingly leafy East London garden.

TIM BURTON
FANTASY

Everything about David Carter's style is carefully considered and refined. His home is like a darkly witty Tim Burton fantasy—full of wit, charm, and character, and with nothing out of place.

He has a very pretty housemaid who tiptoes around brandishing a feather duster. She is clad in the traditional Victorian housemaid's uniform of black dress and white pinafore and hat. And whenever I pass by for a cup of tea, David seems to have an endless stream of Botticellli-style female artisans painting or gilding his walls to make real the new ideas David has just had that week.

We have always shared the romantic notion that one day we would team up together in a creative sense. With our design ethos, we are sure we would create something life-altering in the world of interior decoration.

At one time we even flirted with the idea of having our own decorating show on TV. To discuss our prospective project, David took me to dine at his regular haunt, The Wolseley in Piccadilly. Now it is important for mere mortals to understand that, in order to get a table at The Wolseley, one has to book at least a month in advance; but in the case of Mr Carter, a table is permanently reserved just in case he wants it. The artist Lucien Freud was afforded the same honor and he happened to be seated opposite us there that night, enquiring via the Maître d' who the strikng Mr Carter was.

The TV show was put on ice to enable me to write this book. Meanwhile David has taken the world by storm, turning the two top bedrooms of his house into the most seductive and smallest hotel in the world—40 Winks (see pages 182–7).

Above A beautiful hand-painted chest of drawers in this Barry Lyndon-style room overflows with "in-case-of-girlfriend" clothes. Part of David's antique wig and hat collection looks on bemused.

Opposite Mr David Carter's paneled boudoir houses a fabulous Empire bed and canopy that look as if they have just

THE HEDONISTIC HAVEN
A CHILD'S DREAM

One year, on a romantic summer holiday, I was taken to dine at L'Ambroisie in Paris. There I spotted the restaurant's magnificent antique marble floors, inlaid with clover-leaf details in black slate.

Together with a trip to Italy, that visit provided the inspiration for a commission I had recently undertaken with the outrageously brilliant architect, Mr David Bristow. We were to decorate a London house for a couple who were in the throes of love. The young and very passionate pair were so romantically inclined that, although they wanted their house to be a family home first and foremost, they also dreamed of making it a seductive, fairytale, hedonistic haven.

Many years later, their handsome mansion has seen six beautiful children come into the world and doubtless has many a tale to tell.

Right Here in the intoxicatingly seductive dining room, I laid the floors with reclaimed Jerusalem stone with a slate inlay, inspired by the stone floors of the Parisian restaurant, L'Ambroisie. I found the carved stone fireplace at a salvage yard. The room is lit by a huge window together with the log fire, an iron chandelier, and gilded wall sconces. When the table is not commandeered for dining, it plays host to books on art and literature, a decorative birdcage, and an antique cut-velvet shawl. Boxwood and ferns edge the room.

Above A painted armoire houses the kitchen sink, a food preparation area, and a stock of homemade and bought gourmet delights. Painted by Miss Jayne Pope, the armoire has Dante Gabriel Rossetti-style ladies on its door fronts. The gilded metalwork chandelier merges overhead with branches of contorted willow while below, the floor is made of antique terracotta.
Opposite The Aga sits in the chimneybreast with a surround made from a Venetian doorway. The whiskey-colored walls give the room a warm glow.

Above In this glorious reading room, the walls were inspired by the paintings of the Sistine Chapel and were executed by Miss Jayne Pope in shades of

THE MARBLE ANGEL
FOUNTAIN ROOM

Above I found this marble angel at Lassco, a renowned architectural salvage store, and then commissioned the terra-cotta arch to surround it. With the addition of the huge conch shell, it has become a fountain. I decorated the area around the angel with flints and oyster shells. Every morning at 3am I would drive to the back of seafood restaurant Quaglino's, where they had kindly saved me last night's empty oyster shells. I then had to bury them at the back of my garden for six months to get rid of the rather pungent smell!

Left The Victorian daybed is cloaked in a delectable chinoiserie shawl and dotted with my Foxy Cushions. It beckons one to rest in front of the double doors opening onto the orchard. Vintage "vellum" luggage serves as coffee tables and the antique oak floorboards are laid in a herringbone pattern. The classic three-tiered, hand-painted, Fortuny silk lamp was bought in Venice.

Above Silk dupion lined with old velvet is made into curtains that I use as bed hangings and window curtains. The two carpet-covered chairs are a market find and I found the marble chimneypiece in Paris and adorned it by stacking fresh lavender on top.

Opposite The armoire has been gilded and aged by Miss Jayne Pope. The dressing table, chairs, and chandelier were rescued from

THE
COPPER
BATHROOM

The magnificent copper bathtub
that is the centerpiece of this
room was being sold as junk in
Brick Lane Market. All it needed
was a good spit and polish.

Together with a Welsh lady
artisan called Eunice, I handmade
the pebble and fossil floor. The
curtains are made from vintage
paisley fabric, the lantern is
Middle Eastern, and the doors
to the bathroom are Victorian
stained glass.

SEDUCTIVE JOURNEYS
& RENDEZVOUS

THE
PRIVATE JET

THE
KARMA CAB

THE HON GREG PIGGOT'S
BARGE

A ROMANTIC DINNER AT
JULIE'S

HIGH TEA AT
COCOMAYA

THE
PRAIRIE

40 WINKS
THE TWO-BEDROOM
HOTEL

THE PRIVATE JET

My fantasy private jet, which takes me around the world at the drop of a hat, looks just as Chocolate Towers looks on any given day.

The jet has elements of all my inspirations of the moment. Antique African hangings from the Congo adorn the doorways and floors, while my leopard skin and sequin Foxy Cushions sit on the chairs, all creating a glamorous yet relaxed feel.

I also found a pair of French 1930s sequined jackets that I made into delicate lampshade to add some soft lighting.

In this luxurious atmosphere, any journey would be serene and calm.

Left Luscious red roses, in vases that are screwed into the tables, scent the air throughout this oasis-like journey.

THE
KARMA KAB

There is only one truly seductive way of motoring around this crazy town of ours and that is in a Karma Kab. These were invented by my guru and Rabbi, Tobias Moss, who brought a fleet of 1950s Bristol cars from India one year and decorated them like sets from a Bollywood movie.

Strong Indian incense fills the air, the springy seats are covered in wedding saris, one's feet rest on Rhajastani carpets, and the roofs are covered with hand-applied mosaic made from broken pieces of china and mirror.

Above Toy decorations from India sit on the dashboard with lovely flower offerings and a statue of Ganesh.

Right A "raving beauty" dressed in a Pam Hogg catsuit arrives in the back of a Karma Kab.

Rabbi Tobias Moss carpeted the dashboard and steering
wheel with trimmings made from Indian curtains, upholstery
braid, and tasseled fringes.

The springy backseats and interior of the roof are heavily
decorated with saris, jewels, and beads. Fuchsia pink pansies
dot the space and a sequined lantern glows down on the scene.

THE HON
GREG PIGGOT'S BARGE

Around the corner from where I live is one of the most glorious areas in London—Little Venice. Along its canals floats the delightful 1930s barge of my dear friend and producer of experimental theater, The Hon Gregory Piggot.

Gregory is part of a large group of boatspeople known as the "Water Gypsies" because they have no fixed mooring and move every couple of weeks. Not long ago I had dinner with him on his boat in Camden; the time before that it was moored in Regent's Park. His is a traveler's lifestyle. It is one that only a certain type of person can handle; Gregory takes it all in his stride.

Nowadays his is a one-man boat with a wood-burning stove and an old diesel engine room. The boat's interiors are as handsome and strong as Gregory is himself. The mahogany-lined walls and oil-burning lamps on board create a feeling of artistic reverie and an intense calm. I added draped deep burgundy silk throws and an abundance of turn-of-the-century textiles to cover every possible sittable surface. Books on art, literature, and poetry line the bookshelves, and the kettle whistles out to tell you that the water's boiling. It's hard to believe that Gregory's living quarters once housed the cargo that used to be carried up and down the Grand Union Canal.

Gregory sleeps in the traditional boatsman's cabin at the stern where at one time a family of four would have eaten, cooked, and slept. His bed is tucked away in a mahogany closet by day, but by night it miraculously unfolds.

With nothing more than a radio to belt out classical music and neighboring boatspeople as company, this raw and rugged but sensuous home is as seductive and rebellious toward the modern world as it gets.

Right The Hon Greg's kitchen is lit by oil lamps and natural daylight.

Overleaf A glimpse through to Greg's galley. I draped velvet throws and Foxy Cushions on the wine-colored velvet deep-buttoned sofa. The rug is a sequin-edged Indian textile. Burning candles light the way.

THE WOOD-BURNING STOVE

Above Framed family photographs decorate the walls.
Left A wood-burning stove heats the barge and boils endless kettles of water.

Overleaf Greg's bed awash with velvets, silks, and tapestries provides an almost Dickensian
scene. Traditional barge paintings adorn the walls and a copy of Roland Barthe's *A Lover's*

AT JULIE'S

I have always had a mad crush on Julie's Restaurant. I was first taken there when I was eighteen on a romantic date with my first love. We parked in a sleepy avenue in Notting Hill Gate and were shown down a dark, rickety stairwell to the basement of what seemed to be a bewitchingly private Victorian home.

What we had stumbled into was a treasure trove of intimate dining rooms all mysteriously cloaked in an abundance of lace and antique damask curtains. Some tables were draped with linen and some with fringed vintage shawls. The walls were covered with antiquated peeling wallpapers and Rococo mirrors and the soft, gentle lighting was provided by a collection of 1930s beaded wall-lights dotted around the rooms, by glowing candelabras, and by the roaring open fire. There were deep, baggy, faded velvet sofas to loll in before and after dinner, and richly carved Indian doorways.

I remember sitting with the singer Marvin Gaye on one side of me and the dress designer Ossie Clarke on the other. We were all listening to Fleetwood Mac and Santana's *Moonflower* being played on the stereo and were watching the beautiful women of the 1970s float by wearing chiffon maxi dresses, baggy boots, and scarves tied around their wide-brimmed hats.

Julie's hasn't changed much at all. It's still a deeply romantic, secluded place to dine at and be courted in on a night of dreams.

Above A vase Philip Sallon bought me from a garage sale has made its way to one of the tables at Julie's.
Opposite My god daughter Olivia Ravden reading at a table draped with a Chinese shawl. Fairy lights and candles light her wa

Overleaf The conservatory and Victorian cast-iron spiral staircas are whitewashed and I used faded pinkish-yellow roses and crean church candles to give the room a subtle contrast of sorts. The parasol on the floor shields Olivia's pale skin from the summer sun

BURNING WITH DESIRE
LOG-FIRE ROOM

Above I found these faded 1970s mustard-colored feathers in a flea
market and dotted them at random among the flowers in the stone urns
all around the restaurant.

Opposite A pair of carpet-covered directors' chairs flank a roaring fire
with an antique kelim at their feet.

Preceding Page These rooms in the restaurant feature a wild melange
of Turkish rugs, French tapestry, fringed Victorian shawls, and Venetian silks
and velvets. Vegetation pours out of an oversized stone urn and oriental
bric-a-brac rules.

HIGH TEA AT COCOMAYA

My local tea house is owned by a couple of outstandingly charming friends of mine, Joel Bernstein and Walid al Damirji. From the moment we walk through the door, my guest and I are utterly mesmerized. It's like stepping into an enchanted forest where the most sumptuous of picnics awaits us.

The furniture is an intelligent collection of antique and modern pieces. The wonderful 1920s display cabinets and chunky wooden chairs have been insightfully painted a glossy sharp cherry red color. The two rows of overhead porch lamps that flirt over the sundries, show off their funky naked lightbulbs, while their electric cables are tastefully wrapped in cherry-colored velvet. The rest of the shop is lit only by candles that drip into an array of vintage porcelain and ceramic candlesticks.

One table is heaving with handmade chocolates, artistic pastries, and fresh fruit tarts that are lovingly made in the kitchen at the back. The other is flanked by half a dozen of the sharp cherry-painted chairs. As we sit down to be served handcut sandwiches and perfumed jasmine tea poured out of exquisite antique china teapots, I feel as if I am sitting in a particularly stylish person's front parlor.

Leaning casually around the shop are magnificent etched-glass and mirrored doors rescued from old hotels. Cocomaya is a midsummer's night dream, the "purrfect" meeting place to have tea and a slice of lemon cake, and see where the afternoon takes you.

Right A devastatingly beautiful collection of antique china cups displayed like the tulips in a Delft tulip vase.
Opposite An etched-glass circa 1930 door rescued from the Dorchester Hotel stands next to a louvered French armoire filled with chocolate shoes and odd teapots and candelabras.

Overleaf Olivia ponders her tea and freshly made pastries against a backdrop of glass and light. Cocomaya was going to be The Pelican Cafe, hence the magnificent painting of a pelican by Andy Regan.

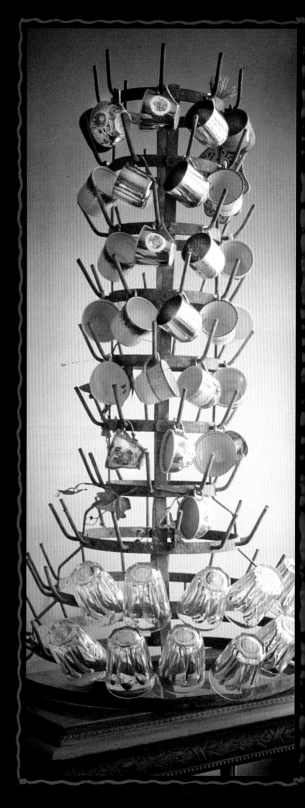

Dorchester
Grill
Breakfast
Luncheon
Dinner

THE PRAIRIE
RACHEL ASHWELL

all so unpremeditated. She apparently has no [...] the effect she creates.

Not long ago Rachel realized her dream and b[...] 100-year-old ranch that she has turned into th[...] seductive B&B imaginable. Simply called *The Pra[...] 180 miles from Austin Texas (how raw is that?) S[...] middle of the famed Round Top Flea [...] community and standing in 46 acres of astou[...] beautiful land, *The Prairie* has seven heavenly [...] Chic Couture-decorated houses.

Ever since I stumbled into Rachel Ashwell's Shabby Chic Couture shop in New York, I fell hook, line, and sinker in love with this inspirational US brand. All the squidgy loose-covered armchairs and insanely comfortable baggy sofas had vintage silk flowers pinned on their brown-paper label price tickets. Now that's what I call style! I then saw Pamela Anderson's Malibu home. It was decked out from head to foot in Shabby Chic Couture's furnishings. Pammy lolled around on the sofas in cut-off jeans and very little else. I was truly blown away. Rachel's other clients, to name but a few, include Julia Roberts, Bruce Willis, and Bruce Springsteen. I just had to meet the creator of these inspired ideas.

Everything in them is all that Rachel stands for [...] authenticity, her admiration of the bea[...] imperfection, and her unadulterated apprecia[...] luxury. I can think of very few places that [...] devastatingly drop-dead romantic as this on[...] wouldn't bat an eyelid if Paul Newman cycled p[...] Robert Redford stopped by for a horse ride. Yea[...] Rachel girl is top of my tree!

Above Left The sitting and sleeping room in Blue Bonnet Bar[...] is whimsically primitive. The oversized loose-covered sofa mak[...] for "beauty, comfort, and function." It is complemented by dain[...] vintage chairs covered in floral silk found in the flea market an[...] lovingly restored.
Below Left The gorgeous Rachel Ashwell.
Opposite Upstairs at Liliput Lodge. Built in 1880 and the [...] original house on the property, it came with mellow blue-pain[...] woodplank walls. The beautifully imperfect patched curtains se[...] the stage. A gently peeling bed and extra sleeping space for ea[...] flea-market shoppers are sumptuously dressed in Rachel's luxu[...] Shabby Chic Couture bedding.

So, when Rachel Ashwell's Shabby Chic Couture furnishings shop opened in London's Notting Hill Gate,

the first thing I did was to invite Rachel out to lunch. We inevitably hit it off and have since become great friends and confidantes.

English by birth, Rachel looks as if she has walked straight out of the Scott Cooper movie *Crazy Heart*. She wears faded jeans loosely slung on her hips, worn-in cowboy boots, and vintage shirts. Everything about this woman is sexy. The most sexy thing of all, however, is that it is

Overleaf Left Love on the Range. *The Prairie* hosts romantic [...] weddings in faded grandeur style thanks to Rachel's personal [...] collection of props and frills. This papier-mâché wedding cake h[...] graced many a wedding (including one of Pammy's in Las Vegas[...] An abundance of frills and flowers offset the corrugated tin ro[...] and the old wood walls.
Overleaf Right Bathing in Blue Bonnet Barn. A crisp white sho[...] curtain and fluffy white towels complement the claw-foot tub [...] the old plank floor, complete with grafitti from the last century[...] romance indeed.

40 WINKS
THE TWO-BEDROOM HOTEL

40 Winks is the whimsically glamorous, two-bedroom hotel owned by the impresario Mr David Carter (see page 126). He sometimes holds the most delightful evenings there, inviting a select few to dress up in p.j.'s and negligees, and lounge around his home listening to bedtime stories recited by some of London's intellectuals. David is one of those real characters who give the English the soubriquet "eccentric."

Opposite The bathroom in the famous two-bedroom hotel *40 Winks*. A huge double-ended brass bathtub awaits with "your slippers, sir."

Overleaf Left Net pompoms hang like a chandelier in the drawing room. The corseted 1950s dress has a petticoat made of several layers of stiff tulle.
Overleaf Right A Madame Récamier scenario at the other end of the drawing room includes elegant embroidered silks and satins, a buttoned Empire-style sofa, and muted paneled walls. All in contrast to the contemporary vibe found opposite.

Above A pile of 1920s "vellum" suitcases and a hatbox sit beneath a nautical Rude Lampshade that David commissioned me to make for him.

Opposite A mannequin dressed in a tulle petticoat and black embroidered Spanish apron oversees the 1930s mirrored cabriole-legged dressing table

SERA'S
HOUSE JEWELS

I began making my Rude Lampshades and Foxy Cushions from home with my Miss Moneypenny, aka Mrs Maureen Baker, when my children were young. Mrs Baker served her apprenticeship with the fashion designer Hardie Amies and became a fully-fledged tailoress in 1959. Maureen's work is second to none. I truly cherish the day our paths crossed.

I often wander through the markets to find wonderful old antique damask lace or faded silk curtains for my Foxy Cushion and Rude Lampshade collections. Some of the wonderful array of exquisite textiles that I bring home are lovingly handmade into cushions and loosely stuffed. I have been known occasionally to slip a handful of fresh lavender inside the stuffing before the cushions are sewn up and finished. And I often trim the cushions with leftover ribbons from my Rude Lampshades.

I began making these because I could never find beautiful enough lampshades to put in my customers' homes. Lampshades were always my thing: as a child I would drape fringed silk scarves over my mother's plain shades—a habit I still indulge in today whenever I stay in a hotel. The secret of the Rude Lampshades lies in their hand-dyed linings. They give even the most sallow complexion an "I'm in love" glow!

INDEX

ACKNOWLEDGMENTS

To John Fossey for all your love and support ... I will never forget.

To the photographer Gisela Torres for her outstanding interior photography throughout most of this book.

To Meryl for all her assisting and retouching work.

To Shani Joel for her invaluable help.

To Matt, who put all this pretty mumbo jumbo together on a computer.

It was a sheer honor to work with you all on *Seductive Interiors*.

A heartfelt thank you to my "behind the scene" stars and hidden heroes of *Seductive Interiors*.

To Mrs Maureen Baker, who makes all the beautiful Foxy Cushions and Rude Lampshades.

To Miss Jayne Pope who is the absolute mistress of fine art painting and gilding.

To Mr Evandro Kuhn, a member of the Guild of Master Craftsmen, for his wicked upholstery work.

Thank you all for the fantastic years we have worked together. You are like my family. Thank you for your first-class impeccable work throughout and superb sense of humor most of the time!

CREDITS

For all interior decoration commissions of the exquisite, beautiful, cozy, homey, loving, fun, seductive, bohemian, and chilled kind, please do not hesitate to contact me.

Sera Hersham Loftus

Seductive Interior decorations by www.seraoflondon.com

Rude Lampshades, Foxy Cushions, exotic make-up for walls by www.seraoflondon.com

Thank you to all those who allowed me to photograph their interiors:

Rachel Ashwell's Shabby Chic Couture www.rachelashwellshabbychiccouture.com

Ballerina, interior decorator, and choker maker, Naomi Tate www.naomitatedesigns.com

Femme fatale, singer, and dancer, Frances Ruffelle www.francesruffelle.com

Pop sensation and raving beauty, Eliza Doolittle www.elizadoolittle.com

Actress and designer, Sadie Frost www.frostfrench.com

Make-up artist for Sadie Frost natashabethdavies@gmail.com

The impresario, David Carter www.alacarter.com

Actress and performer, Esmé www.esmeforever.com

The most sensational hatmaker, Victoria Grant www.victoriagrant.co.uk

My lovely client and now friend, Nina Gill

The beautiful Lily-India

The wonderful Greg Piggot; during the making of this book, Greg Piggot sadly passed away, leaving a truly admirable reputation and loving memories with all who knew him

For romantic journeys:

Tobias Moss' Karma Kabs www.karmakabs.com

Private jet www.shootaviation.co.uk

For romantic rendezvous:

Julie's Restaurant and Champagne Bar www.juliesrestaurant.com

Cocomaya, fine chocolatier and artisan bakery www.cocomaya.co.uk

The Prairie by Rachel Ashwell www.theprairiebyrachelashwell.com

40 Winks www.40winks.org

Thanks also to:

Mr Philip Sallon, Art Director

For magical photography www.giselatorres.co.uk

The top upholstery man www.ekdesignlondon.co.uk

Photos of beautiful women by www.louisebobbe.com

For alternative fires, Cathy Azria at www.bd-designs.co.uk

Balustrades and ironwork, Andrew Findlay www.andrew-findlay.com

Tasteful and romantic flower displays, Divine Flowers www.divine-flowers.co.uk

Location hire www.airspaces.co.uk

The queen of retouching www.meryldavies.com

Design and artworking www.nineteen-creative.co.uk

Additional photography:

Photography on pages 9 and 90–91, copyright © Joel Anderson www.joelanderson.com

Photography on back cover and page 4, copyright © Clive Arrowsmith www.clivearrowsmith.com

Photography on pages 84–87 and page 189, copyright © Darren Chung www.darrenchung.com

Photography on page 88, copyright © David Hindley Photography www.davidhindley.com; tel +44 (0) 7973 492036

Photography on pages 136–145, copyright © Mark Luscombe White www.markluscombewhyte.com; www.ewastock.com

Photography on page 17, copyright © Julian Marshall www.julianmarshall.com

Photography on front cover, pages 10–12, 18–19, and 66, copyright © Michael Paul www.michaelpaulphotography.co.uk

Photography on page 189, copyright © Ray Shore

Photography on pages 14–16, copyright © Colin Streater www.colinstreater.com, with styling by Philip Sallon

Photography on page 178 (portrait of Rachel Ashwell), copyright © Caroline True www.carolinetrue.com

Photography on pages 134–135, copyright © Simon Upton www.simonupton.com

Illustration and artwork

Painting on page 70 by Maggi Hambling www.maggihambling.com

Portrait of Sadie Frost on page 94 by Jake and Dinos Chapman www.jakeanddinoschapman.com

Portrait of Sadie Frost and Jemima French on page 96 by Tim Watkins, represented by Début Art

Every effort has been made to contact copyright holders and acknowledge sources, but the publishers would be glad to hear of any omissions.